GW00645067

HARD THINKING
The Fusion of Politics & Science

Herbert E. Meyer

Storm King Press
Friday Harbor, Washington

Storm King Press books are available at special discounts for bulk purchases for sales, promotions, premiums, fund raising or non-profit educational use.

For details contact:

Storm King Press
PO Box 2089
Friday Harbor, WA 98250
Tel: (206) 378-3910

Cover by Teutschel Design Services

Manufactured in the United States

ISBN: 0-935166-08-4

This book is for Gordon J. MacDonald, who helped me to understand, and for Charles M. Lichenstein, who helped me pull it all together.

Also by Herbert E. Meyer

The War Against Progress, 1979
How to Write
  [co-authored with Jill M. Meyer], 1986
Real-World Intelligence, 1988

Contents

"Hard thinking is thinking about particulars or thinking in terms or language that can convey a clear and precise meaning to other people; putting forward ideas which can be tested, which can be the subject of critical examination; statements that make an intellectual appeal as opposed to a visceral appeal—if you admit the distinction. Soft thinking is thinking that makes an appeal to or through the emotions; which gives one a nice cozy feeling inside; which attempts to persuade one of what ought to be intellectual truths by non-intellectual means."

Peter Medawar
My Life in Science *(1966)*

The first time a routine business trip changed my life was when I chanced to meet the woman who is now my wife. The second time was when business took me to a country I had never been to before — had never even thought about visiting — but which utterly captured my fancy.

Of course I hadn't enough time to explore the new country properly, so after returning home I did the only sensible thing: I found some excuse to make another visit. This second visit left me even more intrigued. How was it that a country so absolutely fascinating — successful, vibrant, extraordinarily literate — received so little attention in my own land? As best I could tell, none of my friends or business associates had ever been there. Or if they had, the country apparently had made little impression on them because they never thought it worth talking about.

I set out to learn everything I could about this newly discovered land: its history, its geography, its people, above all its culture. I scoured new and used bookstores for anything published about the country, and was amazed to find so many good books available; obviously they had always been there but I just hadn't noticed them. I began to learn the language, then subscribed to the country's leading magazines. Despite my language problems these magazines were a joy to read; articles were clear, insightful, on average vastly better written than articles in my own country's leading publications. Soon I was inventing excuses to return. With each trip I spent longer on the ground, always delaying my return voyage home to the last possible moment.

Now, when a man loses interest in going home there is usually a reason for it. In this case the trouble at home wasn't personal but public. Everything seemed to be going wrong at once: our economy was stagnant, our education system was a shambles, racial tensions were rising, our cities were crumbling, our health care system was collapsing, our technological base had atrophied, our commercial vitality had drained out.

But, as serious as they were, these problems were dwarfed by a vastly more serious problem: we had lost our national talent for solving problems. Not that we were ignoring them; quite the opposite, in fact. Newspapers, magazines, television shows and radio broadcasts were devoting more space and time to public affairs than ever before. Indeed, we were fairly bombarded by articles and discussions of each specific national ailment. Here and there, to be fair about it, some elected official, interest-group spokesperson, scholar or commentator would put forth an important fact, a new idea, an analysis that provided a clear perspective, even a deep insight that pointed the way toward a workable solution.

But now, more than ever before, these facts, ideas, analyses and insights were buried beneath an avalanche of nonsense, baloney, ideological posturing and outright lies. The result was a form of national confusion that came from being unable to see any problem clearly: to understand its causes, to evaluate its present condition, to identify its indicators and to tell if they were pointing up or down, to judge whether any particular situation was growing worse or getting better. In short order this confusion — this unprecedented, impenetrable intellectual fog — had disoriented us so completely that our sense of national direction was utterly gone. We began to wander aimlessly, which only made our problems grow worse. The national mood became clinically depressed, even dangerous. Appallingly but not surprisingly, more and more people came to conclude that our country's day was done; that after so many extraordinary national triumphs we had become caught in a downward, perhaps irreversible national spiral.

To be sure, the other country I had discovered also had its problems, and they were every bit as complex and as serious as those at home. But — and this is what had so captured and held my fancy — this other country had developed an approach to solving its problems that really worked. It was an orderly, rational approach that made our own efforts look chaotic and even childish. Indeed, the more I watched this other country move forward, the more painful and frustrating it was to watch my own country spin its wheels and go nowhere.

As my trips abroad became ever more frequent, my friends and business associates began to notice that my mind was now on something, or rather some place, else. How could they not have noticed? My attendance at professional conferences and seminars became less frequent, and when I did show up I tended to blather on about the way our counterparts in the other country were coping with their problems. My colleagues listened politely, but it was clear they had no idea what I was talking about and little interest in learning.

Before long I had become a drop-out, not in the sense of growing a beard and making a living by selling herbal teas or birds carved from driftwood, but in the sense of ceasing to play the role that my professional credentials and status allowed and instead going off in a wholly different direction. But even this wasn't enough. My frustration with our way of working things out — or, rather, of not working things out — finally reached the point where I began to toy with the idea of getting out entirely, of emigrating from my country to the other one. Of course, this was an absolutely crazy idea. I could barely speak the language, despite my efforts to learn it. My professional credentials weren't at all transferable, so the prospect of ever reaching my current professional status — or my current income — was virtually non-existent. Yet the less practical sense it made to emigrate the more I found myself thinking about it. I couldn't help myself. Increasingly, I had begun to feel like a foreigner in my own country, while more and more the new one felt like home.

This new country does not belong to the United Nations, and you won't find it on any map. That's because it isn't a geographic place at all, but an intellectual world. It is Science, and it is as real and remarkable a place as I have ever been. And instead of "emigrating" I have decided to remain where I am — in the intellectual world of politics, if you will — and to help change this intellectual world by importing what is best in the other world's culture, specifically its approach to solving problems and resolving contentious issues.

More precisely, I believe that the business of our public affairs can be put back on track — not only here in the United States, but throughout the world — by adopting key aspects of the scientific culture. Indeed, I believe that adoption of the scientific culture is vital if we are to cope with the global public problems and issues that confront us right now, and with the ones that will confront us in the years and decades that lie ahead.

Science is a great many things, and I have called them a great many names; but in the end they all return to this: science is the acceptance of what works and the rejection of what does not. This needs more courage than we might think.

Jacob Bronowski
The Common Sense of Science *(1951)*

L et me jump immediately to the point: The fundamental difference between science and politics is that in science, results count and being right matters. It could not be otherwise, because the scientific method itself rests upon the sequence of idea, experiment and observation: of proposing a thesis, then systematically trying one alternative after another, rejecting what doesn't work and accepting what does, no matter how it goes against one's original idea or personal prejudices.

It is what happens next that makes Science so remarkable. When a scientist comes up with what he or she believes is a new discovery or a new insight into nature that shatters the existing paradigm — Einstein's theory of relativity, for instance, or Watson & Crick's revelation of the DNA double-helix — this purported discovery or insight is subjected to serious and critical evaluation by other scientists. The key word here is evaluation, which is not the same as comment. When scientists are presented with a new theory they don't jump in to say what they think, or what they feel, about it. They roll up their sleeves to actually test it. After all, the true test of any purported insight is its ability to accurately and reliably predict; to predict, for example, that if you combine two atoms of hydrogen with one atom of oxygen, the result always will be one molecule of H_2O, or water. This means that any claim to a new insight or discovery must contain within it something, or some result, that can be measured or replicated.

Sometimes validation comes quickly, for example when the new discovery or insight can easily be replicated by other scientists in their own laboratories. The double-helix structure of DNA, for instance, was immediately seen to be correct by other biologists. In other cases validation comes slowly. Einstein published his famous paper on the Special Theory of Relativity, in which he asserted that a clock at the earth's equator would run slower than one positioned at one of the earth's poles, in 1905; it wasn't until 1955 that clocks could be calibrated to a thousand millionth of a second, which enabled H. J.

Hay to actually prove that Einstein's seemingly bizarre theory was correct. Charles Darwin proposed his theory of evolution in 1857, and while the core of his theory has long since been validated, even now scientists are struggling to refine some aspects of it.

Only when a new theory proves to be valid — when its predictions can be both replicated and measured by others — does that theory becomes accepted as the new truth. And Science respects the truth. More precisely, once a new theory or insight has been validated, those who continue to resist or reject the evidence are pushed aside. Their books and articles cease to be published, their lectures are unattended, their presence at professional conferences no longer sought after. Throughout every corner of a scientific discipline, ideas and perceptions that have been shown to be wrong are set aside; you will not find any university, anywhere, whose chemistry faculty teaches that the air contains phlogiston or whose biology faculty teaches that human intelligence is determined by the shape of one's skull.

As for those who get it right in Science — well, they get Nobel prizes. Those of their colleagues who catch on early to the new theory, and who help evaluate and refine the original insight or discovery, get the key academic and research positions; they control the conferences and seminars, and it is their books and articles that publishers seek. At universities throughout the world it is their insights and discoveries that students are taught. In sum, their reality becomes the one upon which that particular discipline moves forward — and upon which the next advances and the next technologies will be based — until another scientist comes up with a new insight or discovery that once again shatters the paradigm and starts up the process all over again.

It would be a mistake to romanticize Science. The image of scientists as selfless human beings dreaming only of a better world, dressed in white coats and fairly humming to themselves in their labs as they peer into their microscopes or pour some frothing concoction from one test tube into another, is vivid but not accurate. In many ways science is a grubby, rough-and-tumble, ferociously competitive business where the next year's budget is fought over as viciously as in the marketing division of any multinational company. And, alas, some of the nastiest bastards I have ever met have been scientists. Finally, no profession is perfect and science is hardly an exception. Good people get hurt, good ideas get knocked around or buried, horrible errors of judgment and terrible injustices do happen

But it would be even more foolish not to look beyond these imperfections to those features of the scientific culture that make it unique and that have contributed so much to its success. First, Science is a true democracy in that it will seriously consider any new idea, no matter who first proposes it or how nutty it seems. Second, Science is self-correcting in that any promising thesis which turns out to be false is always, in the end, exposed; any attempt at outright fraud, for instance by skewing experimental results, invariably will be discovered when other scientists try to replicate the original research. Third, science is self-renewing: all scientists recognize and accept that there is no such thing as final truth, that each step forward is merely that until yet another insight comes along to overturn the one before. The very essence of Science is that its truths are cumulative.

Even the most casual tourist to Science is struck by the working environment — the public mood, if you will — these cultural features create. Whatever their individual personalities and personal shortcomings, all scientists share an insatiable curiosity to understand how the world works — not how it ought to work or how they would like it to work, but how it really does work. And so, despite the natural and often ferocious competition that permeates their daily work, there is among scientists an extraordinary sense of enthusiasm and shared enterprise. What drives scientists forward is the hope of adding just one more piece to the puzzle, of coming just one step closer to genuine understanding. They honor the truth, and those who find it, as well as those who seek it honestly but fail. And because they are all working toward the same goal, they celebrate any individual's triumph as a victory for the entire enterprise. This attitude gives rise to what the great scientist and writer Jacob Bronowski calls a sense of the future: a driving, pounding optimism that comes from the faith that things can and will get better because honorable people are working together, to learn and to share a growing body of knowledge, for the sheer pleasure and triumph of getting it right.

Because Science is so much like a foreign country, those of us who stumble across its borders tend to assume that, like a real country, it has developed naturally and, so to speak, has been there forever. But it turns out that Science isn't natural at all. As the anthropologist Loren Eisley has written, "This much at least we know: science among us is an invented cultural institution, an institution not present in all societies, and not one that may be counted upon to arise from human instinct....Science is not natural to man at all. It has to be learned, consciously practiced, stripped out of the sea of emotions, prejudices, and wishes in which our daily lives are steeped."

The invention and development of science is itself a fascinating subject. In the ancient world only Greece developed an approach that embraced the sequence of idea, experiment and observation. In the modern world it was the scientific revolution in Europe that ran from about 1500 to roughly 1700 that gave western civilization its edge and that, while men elsewhere continued to believe in what Eisley calls "uninhibited dreams and fantasies," powered the West forward through a series of scientific and technological advances. So it isn't by chance that western civilization has produced more scientists than all other civilizations combined. Rather, it is because western civilization, more than its counterparts, developed the rules of Science and then consciously set out to assure itself a steady flow of scientists by codifying these rules and teaching this culture to generation upon generation of students through the formal process of education.

Today the achievements of Science are so much a part of our lives that we tend to ignore the obvious: that Science itself may well be history's greatest invention. It's a mistake that scientists rarely make. When asked after a lecture to name his single greatest invention, Thomas Edison stunned his audience by replying, "The research lab." However remarkable may be the products that have emerged from Science — everything from the electric bulb, to the Space Shuttle, to the polio vaccine, to our VCRs and portable CD players — none is as remarkable as the methodology that produced them, and that will continue to produce the new and the wondrous as long as men and women are willing to set aside those "uninhibited dreams and fantasies" and instead to hold rigorously to the sequence of idea, experiment and observation. This is the culture of science, and it is a stunning human achievement, perhaps even a work of art.

If the scientists have the future in their bones, then the traditional culture responds by wishing the future did not exist. It is the traditional culture, to an extent remarkably little diminished by the emergence of the scientific one, which manages the world.

C.P. Snow
**The Two Cultures and the
Scientific Revolution** *(1959)*

Now look at the culture of politics. While Science is the quest for knowledge, politics is the struggle for power. Thus politicians strive for and celebrate not what works, but what wins. When confronted with a new fact or idea the politician's instinct is not to evaluate it objectively, but to determine whether it is immediately useful and, if so, how. Facts and ideas that can be made to be useful will be seized upon — ripped from the womb, so to speak, and hurled into battle like so much intellectual cannon fodder. New facts and ideas judged to be useless will be ignored, deprived of life support and left to die stillborn. And when a new fact or idea comes along that is seriously troublesome or disquieting — for example one that shatters the basis for a present or proposed policy, such as the clearly measurable disemployment effect of every rise in the minimum wage — that fact or idea will be discredited as rapidly and as thoroughly as possible.

It is inevitable that in a culture like this one, intellectual standards will decline. Any culture that has no accepted mechanism for the rigorous evaluation of facts and ideas will inevitably degenerate. Moreover, while politics will certainly attract good people, it will also attract bad people — people who will lower standards rather than uphold them. And declining standards have a momentum of their own; the more they decline the more they decline. At first the good people are the ones who raise standards. Then they are the ones who struggle to maintain standards. Finally they are the ones whose standards are merely declining more slowly than everyone else's.

Let this go on for long enough and the culture itself will lose the ability to think seriously and coherently — to think hard — about a given issue. And when hard thinking is gone, all that remains is what the biologist Peter Medawar calls soft thinking: thinking that makes an appeal to or though the emotions; which gives one a nice cozy feeling inside; which attempts to persuade one of what ought to be intellectual truths by non-intellectual means. This shift, from a culture based on thinking to one based on feeling, is marked by the declining value of objective results — by the abandonment of objectivity itself — and by the rising importance of emotions. The result is what Charles Sykes calls therapeutic politics: "While it remains ostensibly concerned with moral issues, it does not primarily concern itself with what is just or unjust, or even with whether something is true or untrue. These considerations are not irrelevant. But they are overshadowed by concern over 'self-esteem' and 'feelings.' "

Soft thinking leads also to *ideological* politics — the elevation of mythologies, whose approach to the real world may be as remote as communism or as revolting as the racism of the Ku Klux Klan, to the status of touchstones for public policy choices. Ideological politics substitutes incantations for rational debate. Of course not everyone will succumb, either to ideological or to theraputic politics. There will be heros and heroines as well as villains. But in the end a culture always wins.

It is this decline, from hard thinking to soft thinking, that is at the root of our present paralysis and discontent. Soft thinking is so much a part of our political culture now that we scarcely even notice it. Yet each day the press contains literally dozens of examples, from statements by politicians and interest group leaders, to slanted reporting, to newspaper op-ed articles, to the increasingly weird content of our television news shows. My own current favorite example of soft thinking comes from a report in the July 29, 1992 edition of *The New York Times*, on Carol Moseley Braun's campaign for a seat in the U.S. Senate from Illinois. Commenting on the unusual breadth of enthusiasm that Ms. Braun's campaign generated — her subsequent election made her the first black woman in the U.S. Senate — the *Times* provides this quote from an obviously ecstatic (and white) supporter of Ms. Braun: "She's me. She represents everything I feel, everything I want to be. I'm so locked into her that what she says is unimportant." This quote itself would be unimportant, except that it so accurately captures the quality of intellectual analysis that now marks our country's political life. Indeed, intellectual analysis has virtually been replaced by psychobabble.

That this should be happening in the United States right now is depressing but not surprising. If the degradation of a political culture is an inevitable development, it makes sense that as the world's most advanced society we ought to be among the first to reach this sorry stage. But it won't be long before the same intellectual fog that has enveloped us, with its resulting disorientation and policy paralysis, spreads to other democracies and envelops them as well. After all, other countries keep their eyes on us the way members of the Navy's *Blue Angels* airborne acrobatics team keep their eye on the team's lead pilot: if we (or he) fly into the ground so too will everyone else. And if we can pull out in time, they will do likewise.

Only by creating a political culture that parallels the scientific culture will we be able to disperse the intellectual fog in which we are now trapped. That is, we will need to create a political culture based on the sequence of idea, experiment, and observation. It would be a culture in which results count and being right matters, where reality overrides emotion, where policies that fail are set aside no matter how appealing they sound and where policies that succeed are implemented when appropriate no matter who first proposed them and no matter how they go against someone's personal prejudices or someone's armchair prediction of how that policy would work. It would be non-ideological and essentially non-partisan.

The obvious problem is that this sort of culture doesn't fit with human nature. We humans prefer to base our actions on our emotions, our decisions on our feelings. The rigorous sequence of idea, experiment and observation is alien to us. Indeed, this is why the scientific culture is so foreign to so many of us, and why it struggled so hard to take root three centuries ago even among that small band who, in Loren Eisley's apt phrase, "swallowed the bitter pill" of science and so powered western civilization forward. A politics based on the methodology of science will be an even more bitter pill, and to make it work this pill will need to be swallowed by a vastly larger group of people. And they will need to take their doses regularly, forever.

If the idea of a political culture based on the methodology of science strikes you as radical, even as anti-political, that only shows how far gone we are. For it was precisely this idea which excited and guided our country's Founding Fathers when they dreamed up and then created the United States more than two hundred years ago.

By the end of the eighteenth century — remember, the preceding two centuries were those of the Scientific Revolution — the scientific method had already proven itself to be a remarkable success. Thomas Jefferson, Benjamin Franklin and many of their colleagues not only were aware of all this, they were an integral part of it. They studied science; they knew scientists; they did science themselves.

To the Founding Fathers the very idea of democracy was one among many ways of implementing the principles of science, and probably the best. These remarkable men understood that no one, least of all themselves, knew for certain how best to organize and manage a government. Thus the sensible thing to do — the reasonable thing, in this Age of Reason — was to establish a system based upon the proven sequence of idea, experiment and observation; a system that allowed for trial-and-error and for the correction of mistakes, and for structural changes when warranted by circumstance and evidence. To the Founding Fathers, the Congress was analogous to Royal Academies of Science that flourished in England, France and elsewhere on the Continent, in which those who were honored by election would meet to exchange new ideas, create and monitor experiments based on these ideas, then gather to consider the results and the most appropriate actions to take when these results had been analyzed and their implications understood.

The genius of our Founding Fathers is that they knew they didn't have the answers, and so established a system whose very structure and principles would enable the search for answers as mankind developed and became more knowledgeable about how to govern itself. It was no accident that they designed a system of limited and specified powers, reflecting the arduous search for knowledge, and of federalism, which by definition provides a plethora of research labs. When these men referred to the newly independent United States as "an experiment" they meant it more literally than most people today realize.

I have often wondered why highly intelligent people, including many trained in the scientific method and successful in its practice, have a desire to believe in the unbelievable. I suppose it is because they are disillusioned with harsh reality, and seek comfort in the hope that there are powers and forces beyond those outlined in the scientific texts. Reason and evidence provide small hope that the human state can be rapidly and radically improved. Thus the temptation to abandon reason and depend for comfort upon faith.

Donald Gould (1992)

IV

While a case could easily be made that we won't be able to climb back up to the Founding Fathers' standards — God knows each day brings more than enough anecdotal evidence to convince even an optimist that we are too far gone to save — there are two specific and compelling reasons why an effort now just might succeed.

First, as we come to the end of this most politically ideological century, common people around the world — who have borne the brunt of the ideologues — are beginning to set aside whatever doesn't work and to go forward with whatever does, or seems a good bet to do so. The collapse of communism in the Soviet Union and its East European satellites is the most extreme example. The new government in Sweden has put that country's economy back on track by turning sharply away from socialism. In Mexico the economic revitalization led by Carlos Salinas de

Gortari is a triumph of historic proportions, and further south in Argentina common sense at last has begun to take hold. In short, in so many countries the results of ideology have been so visibly horrifying that to ordinary people the idea of trying something that actually will work is more appealing now than it has been for a very long time. The very idea of *doing* what works is in the air.

Second, for the first time in history we have an abundant supply of the raw material that is vital to actually *knowing* what works. Information is the key to understanding, and the ongoing information revolution now provides enough information to conduct our public affairs in a way that has never before been possible. Today literally thousands of the world's best newspapers, magazines and newsletters are available electronically, from the hundreds of database services that compile and make these publications available to anyone with a computer, a modem, and a few hundred dollars a month to spend on access or on-line fees.

Moreover, information correlation software has now reached the market that can scan these newspapers, magazines and newsletters — or any other text — at a rate of several thousand pages per second, searching not merely for key words but for key selected concepts that enable the user to link and correlate related ideas, facts and patterns in ways that have not previously been possible. Not only can researchers now access thousands of pages on a given subject, but now they can sort through these pages thoroughly and efficiently to find whatever they may be looking for. And with today's electronic bulletin boards — thousands already up and running; dozens starting up each month — computer-equipped people interested in a specific subject can trade ideas, data and insights with their colleagues and counterparts literally around the world.

All this, combined with telephones, televisions, radios, and fax machines comprises one of the most spectacular achievements of our age: a global network of electronic information highways whose architecture will seem as wondrous and astonishing a feat to our descendants as the cathedrals of Notre Dame and Chartres seem to us. As those engaged in the business of public affairs learn to travel these information highways as skillfully as their counterparts in science already travel them, they will discover that they are now able to know about, and monitor, any political ideas developed anywhere, along with whatever policies have been implemented on the basis of these ideas.

Just think of what this global reach enables us to do. For example if a state's legislators are debating whether a two percent rise in the sales tax rate would generate more revenues, they can quickly and easily compile information about what actually happened and is happening in every other state whose legislators raised the tax rate.   They can even bring in data from other countries; from Canadian provinces, Swiss cantons or from anywhere else on earth.   Is our Congress debating changes in our nation's health care system? Fine, it is now possible to know about and monitor how health care is provided throughout the world, to compare delivery systems and to determine which features of which systems seem to work best and which do poorly. There is enough information available now to hold an intelligent debate — one based on facts rather than on mere opinions and surmises — and perhaps to design an "experiment" or two and then monitor the results. In education we now can monitor the performances of students in different schools, or school districts, along with the policies of local school boards, to see where students are performing best and then to analyze why. Again, it will be easier now to design "experiments," monitor their results and then reach conclusions based on evidence gathered accurately and over time.

Those engaged in the conduct of public affairs can use today's information systems the way an airplane pilot uses radar: to extend their vision and to display patterns of activity not visible to the naked eye. Of course these information systems will not tell legislators or voters what to do, any more than radar tells an airplane pilot what to do. Rather, these information systems will enable us to know what is actually going on out there, provided that we are willing to search out this information and draw appropriate and accurate conclusions whether we like them or not.

The trick will be to take advantage of information without going overboard.Politics is a unique form of science, and we cannot treat people like lab rats. They are not. But this is not to say that their behavior is wholly unpredictable. For example, given the promise of tangible rewards for hard work, and some assurance that these rewards will be forthcoming on a non-discriminatory basis, most people will be motivated to work hard. Still, there is a big difference between the organization of cells in a body, and the organization of people in a society. Politics goes far beyond mere facts into issues of morals, values, religion and philosophy. These issues matter hugely, sometimes decisively, and well they should. My point is a self-evident one, obvious but impossible to prove: that the more information we have the more likely we will be to make better decisions — provided that we have the wisdom, skill, and courage to use that information honestly and accurately, as scientists rather than as ideologues.

Either one wants to try to understand the world or one does not. If this understanding gives you answers you do not like, that is one of the risks you take.

Lewis Wolpert, 1992

Much of the present disillusionment with politics flows from a perception among quite ordinary, "unscientific" people that their leaders have already fallen behind the curve. And indeed they have. Already there is so much political knowledge available — along with the information-handling and information-correlation technologies needed to manage it all — that a gap has opened between what we are doing and what we are capable of doing. Watching so many of our current policies fail is like watching a sick child die of an infection because his parents believe in witchcraft and won't take him to a pediatrician for a five-dollar dose of penicillin. It is both a tragedy and an outrage. Parents may have the right to believe in whatever weird practices they want, and to ignore the miracles of modern medicine for themselves. But do they have a right to impose these beliefs on their child? Likewise, we all have a right to whatever silly or discredited political views we want; that is the essence of freedom. But do those who are engaged in politics — those who manage or influence the conduct of public affairs — have a right to ignore what we already have learned about the world? When the body politic is ill do those responsible for its welfare have the right to prescribe what amounts to witchcraft?

Look at it this way and the answer is self-evidently no. For right now we have in our hands, or rather within our grasp, enough knowledge to develop and administer better policies than we are now administering. For those who are the victims of these policies — ordinary people (call them "voters") whose lives and hopes are so deeply and directly affected by decisions made by those who manage and influence the conduct of our public affairs — the results are both a tragedy and an outrage. We know too much about key issues — energy, education, crime, health care, the environment, national security and all the rest — to tolerate some of the policies we are now pursuing. We can argue over which policies would be best, in the same way that doctors will argue over which antibiotic may be best suited to a specific infection and specific patient. But just

as today's physicians won't seriously consider
the idea of treating a child's infection by chanting songs while the poor kid lies with his nose
pointed toward Venus, today's politicians have
no right to engage in political witchcraft, to
advocate or embark on policies that make no
sense or have long since been discredited and
surpassed by human knowledge and experience.

Unless we get cracking now this gap which
has opened between what we are doing and what
we are capable of doing — between political
witchcraft and, so to speak, modern political
medicine — will widen. As the information revolution unfolds the amount of knowledge at our
fingertips will expand exponentially. Already
each of us handles more information in a year
than our predecessors a generation ago handled
during their entire careers; and the volume of
information available to us now is but a trickle
compared with the volume that will pour over us
in the years to come. This will include knowledge about our own country, our own people, and
knowledge about other countries and people, and
about their experiences. Increasingly our leaders
will be like doctors with all sorts of wonderful
medicines and diagnostic tools lying around their

labs, but who continue to prescribe the same old snake-oil simply because they haven't taken the time or trouble to open the packages piling up on their desks and to read through the life-saving literature inside.

And this gap not only will widen, it will widen at an accelerating rate. For we are now in the midst of yet another scientific revolution. The breakthroughs being made today in biology, neurology, anthropology, chemistry, physics, astronomy, and in many other fields and disciplines are fundamentally changing our understanding of our world and, perhaps more importantly, of ourselves. Already we have gotten a grasp of how stars and planets come into being, of the internal structure of atoms, of how cells replicate and mutate, even a faint grasp of how the brain stores memory. And it is in our lifetime that human beings first lifted off from earth and began to explore the galaxy. Every day we are learning more about how our species evolved from other species, and how in some cases we have evolved with other species; why we survived and they died out. It is scarcely an exaggeration to say that we are on the verge of simultaneously cracking both the cosmic and the genetic codes; on the threshold of learning how the universe works, and of learning — literally — who and what we are.

Yet those in politics pay no attention as they go about their daily business, arguing over this or that piece of legislation and scrambling to put a spin on the latest perceived gaffe by some candidate or another — or simply chanting their preferred incantations — each convinced that this battle is the most important thing that could possibly be going on in the world. They are oblivious to the goings on in science; its laboratories and its researchers are invisible to them — and, alas, to so many of us. Yet centuries from now, people looking back on this age will consider our political struggles to be trivial compared with our scientific achievements. And the present scientific revolution has nowhere near run its course; the best is yet to come.

The insights and technologies that will flow from these breakthroughs will have an enormous impact on public policy. For example, the more we learn about the human genome — our genetic code, which controls everything from the color of our eyes, to our intellectual and athletic abilities, to the likelihood of our getting cancer — the more we will be able to alter these codes. Will we use this knowledge to cure or prevent diseases, to heighten those genetic traits deemed most desirable, or to "de-select" fetuses whose genome doesn't quite measure up to its parents' wishes? The policy issues here will be legal and moral, and immensely controversial to resolve. Breakthroughs in medicine will reduce the incidence of afflictions such as heart attacks and Alzheimer's disease, which in turn will require changes in Social Security and Medicare programs as people live longer and healthier lives; employment patterns may also need to shift.

Looming before us now are breakthroughs in the earth sciences that will tell us the true causes of acid rain, and that will pin down how quickly the earth really is warming. Thus we will have the knowledge needed to structure environmental policies that will effectively reverse or control these trends. But what will be the impact of these policies on our economies, and on the strategic relationships among nations? Breakthroughs in chemistry and physics not only will affect our psychological and religious perceptions of ourselves and the universe, but will enable the production of new materials, which in turn will give rise to new transportation systems that will affect everything from urban policies to industrial growth to weapons production.

Increasingly our politics will be dominated by the opportunities — and the dilemmas — that will emerge from the revolutions under way now in laboratories around the world. To guide ourselves through all this as safely as possible we will need not only the intellectual firepower to grasp it all, but the intellectual courage — a very different thing — to accept the new knowledge about our world and ourselves that all these breakthroughs will create, and to formulate public policies that will be based on this knowledge rather than on our personal opinions or prejudices. More and more, to be be politically effective we will need to understand science, to be comfortable with scientists, to think like scientists.

We are at a point in human biological and metabiological evolution at which it will be important to know how to improve the quality of the performance of the human mind, not only mentally but emotionally and physically as well. This has deep philosophical and moral, as well as scientific and technical, implications. It has implications for the art of living, the art of meaningful performance in all human endeavors.

Jonas Salk
Anatomy of Reality *(1983)*

VI

It will take time to change our political culture — more time than we would wish. As
Thomas S. Kuhn observes in his seminal work,
The Structure of Scientific Revolutions, when a
paradigm starts to shift those wedded to the
outgoing paradigm tend to resist. In the end they
are defeated rather than persuaded; they are
pushed aside to make room for new people who
are more comfortable with the new perception
and more fluent in its various subtleties. If this
pattern holds for politics, which seems likely,
today's political establishment will need to be
pushed aside. The people who can do it are out
there now, literally in every city and state, fight-
ing lonely and often losing battles. If they can
turn these unconnected battles into a movement,
based on a shared allegiance to the idea of a
politics based on knowledge, they will gain a
collective strength and, eventually, a critical
mass.

Whether this critical mass will develop in a matter of years, or of decades, is impossible to predict. This is one of those cases where it is easier to see how something ultimately will settle out, than to estimate how long it will take to actually happen. But however long may be the gestation period, when the change does come it will happen very quickly. This is the nature of cultural and intellectual revolutions. But such revolutions never just happen by themselves, although it may see that way to those who are most directly affected. They happen because a small group of people made the revolution happen by working at it steadily, silently, sometimes even in stealth. Only when the results are visible to everyone do people look back and discover how long the effort had been under way.

The best place to start this revolution is with our children. We should focus our energies on educating them to understand the difference between soft thinking and hard thinking. Today's children — I mean those younger than 13 — are the most scientifically literate generation ever. It may be true that they watch a lot of garbage on television, but it is also true that they watch a lot of superb shows and series about science such as

Cosmos, Nature, The Infinite Voyage, The Shape of History, or any of David Attenborough's wonderful series such as *Trials of Life* and *Life on Earth*. In addition they gobble up books about science, particularly about dinosaurs, and in toy stores today scientific games and projects fairly fly off the shelves. It shouldn't be too hard to teach the scientific method to these kids — to explain how science came into being and how it powered western civilization forward — and to show them that this kind of orderly, rigorous thinking can be extended to other parts of their lives including public affairs.

More important perhaps, today's children perceive information in a wholly new way. Certainly they are computer-literate in ways the rest of us never will be. They seem to be comfortable with the idea of taking little bits of information from a wide range of sources and then pulling all these bits together into a pattern. Today's children absorb and combine audio, visual and written information better than we do. As they mature these children will grasp the essence and value of information correlation technologies; no doubt they will develop new technologies to handle and sift through even larger volumes of information.

In short, with a bit of guidance today's children may grow up to be more comfortable with the scientific process than we are, and therefore — perhaps — more willing to support those who would use this process as a discipline in public policy formulation.

Our biggest obstacle right now will be the media. With notable exceptions it is corrupt. During the last few years many of the most important news organizations that comprise the popular press have abandoned their vitally important role of informing the public. Instead, these institutions now work to influence the public to support whatever ideas and policies its own journalists and managers support. The press does this by emphasizing whatever issues and facts serve its purposes, while downplaying or even surpressing whatever issues and facts are at cross-purposes to whatever policy objectives the press wishes to achieve. In this sense the press today acts more like a political party than a filter and interpreter of politics; more like one of the teams than the league umpire.

The intellectual corruption of the press is more than a nuisance. It is a catastrophe. It leaves the public blinded, unable to accurately know where we are or what lies directly in front of us. It is as though we are on board a jumbo jet, flying at five hundred miles per hour through a storm, and the radar has gone bonkers. There is no easy solution to the problem of an intellectually corrupt press. It is merely another obstacle that we will need to somehow overcome as we move forward. At least we ought to be aware of how corrupt the popular press has become; then to ignore it when possible, to develop substitutes when feasible and, when necessary, to fight the press head-on with whatever power and resources we can muster.

Ah! Never forget that we can only stave off that fatal degradation if we unite the liberal arts, which embody the sacred fire of sensibility, with the sciences and the useful arts, without which the celestial light of reason will disappear.

> *Bernard Lacepede, closing address to students at the Musee d'Histoire Naturelle, Paris (1802)*

VII

N early four centuries ago a discredited and disheartened English statesman named Francis Bacon turned his attention to the embryonic idea of science. In books such as *The Advancement of Learning* and *Novum Organum* Bacon hammered home his point that experiment and observation were an engine that could carry humanity forward toward the truth. He argued that "We cannot command nature except by obeying her," and in his most famous phrase — "Knowledge is power" — he meant that only through an understanding of how things really work could we seize control of our destinies rather than be at the mercy of forces beyond our control.

The two centuries of scientific progress that Bacon's writing helped to trigger were more than a revolution. Jacob Bronowski argues that they were nothing less than a genetic leap forward — an irreversible step in the cultural evolution of mankind just as radical as the invention of agriculture, or writing, or poetry and art, or urban life. In Bronowski's succinct phrase, "Science is a world view based on the notion that we can plan by understanding." As a result of the leap forward that took place between 1500 and 1700, Bronowski says, "We are committed to a scientific way of thinking and to what it entails, a technological way of acting, and we cannot go back."

The invention of a new political culture — or, if you prefer, the re-invention of our Founding Fathers' political culture — may also prove to be a genetic leap forward in the cultural evolution of mankind. If the idea takes hold fast enough in the United States, and then spreads quickly enough to other countries through today's communications networks, we might be able to reach a critical mass similar to the one which science achieved after 1500 and which enabled the scientific culture to survive and flourish throughout the world, even through some of history's most ghastly political cultures. And if we can achieve such a mass, we may in the end become irreversibly committed to this new political culture just as we are irreversibly committed to science.

I am not suggesting that this new political culture, by itself, would solve any of our current or future problems. There is no such thing as a magic bullet, or a brain-in-a-box that spews out happiness if only one can press the right combination of buttons. Rather, I am suggesting that should we start to conduct our public affairs in a scientific way — based upon the rigorous application of a methodology comprised of ideas, experiments, observations and honest analyses — we will have created an environment in which we are more likely to come up with policies that will work. And if they do — that in itself will spark a revolution with irreversible, indeed irresistible, momentum.

We ought not to have any illusions about all this. Human nature is imperfect, politics is a rough trade, and democracy itself requires the willingness to compromise more often than one likes. Washington will never become merely the world's largest research lab — nor should it. Politics deals with human beings, and we must always be on guard against the social engineer who claims to know what is best for everyone and who, purportedly for the people's own good, would use whatever force may be required to impose that policy on a resisting public. For if there is one thing we have learned from history, surely it is that this attitude leads inevitably to dictatorship.

But just as surely Washington can do better than it is doing now, and it will do better if it adopts the scientific culture. The need is pressing, the information and communications tools lie within our grasp, and the idea itself is in the air. Americans, particularly younger ones, may respond faster and more enthusiastically than most people think. And if the new culture takes hold in the United States it will take hold elsewhere, and keep other countries from going through the same paralysis and discontent that now afflicts us. It may even take hold in some of today's new and fragile democracies, and help them get onto the right track and to stay on that track through the difficult years that lie ahead.

Right now the twentieth century will go down for having produced some of history's worst political ideas, such as communism and fascism. But if, as we approach the end of this century, we can transform politics itself from an individual struggle for power to a collective quest for knowledge about how we can best organize ourselves and manage our public affairs, we may just reverse the equation. Historians looking back on our age would record that in the twentieth century mankind made an irreversible genetic leap. The astounding results of this leap may even lead some historians to suggest that the greatest invention of science isn't science, but politics.

About the Author

Herbert E. Meyer served during the Reagan Administration as Special Assistant to the Director of Central Intelligence and Vice Chairman of the CIA's National Intelligence Council. In these positions he managed production of the U.S. National Intelligence Estimates and other top-secret intelligence projections for the President and his national security advisers. Mr. Meyer is widely credited with being the first senior U.S. Government official to forecast the Soviet Union's collapse, which he did in the early 1980s — to considerable political derision. He later was awarded the National Intelligence Distinguished Service Medal, which is the Intelligence Community's highest honor.

Mr. Meyer's most recent book, *Real-World Intelligence*, is a leading primer on the strategic use of information; it has been published in the U.S., Europe and Asia. In addition to his various business enterprises, Mr. Meyer is a popular speaker at universities and companies throughout the world. He lives with his wife and their two children on San Juan Island in Washington State's Puget Sound.